LEADING WITH CARE

HOLDING AUTHORITY WITHOUT LOSING YOURSELF

LANRE B. OLALEYE

Leading with Care:
Holding Authority Without Losing Yourself

Published by LBO Publishing
McKinney, Texas

ISBN: 979-8-9958150-4-4

Scripture quotations are used for illustrative and reflective purposes.

First Edition, 2026

Dedication

To every leader who refuses to choose between effectiveness and integrity.

This book is for you.

You can lead well, right where you are.

Table Of Contents

Author's Note

Why This Playbook Was Written

The text message arrived at 5:47 PM on a Tuesday.
"I can't do this anymore. I quit."

The sender was one of the most capable leaders I'd ever met - brilliant strategist, strong communicator, deeply committed to excellence. Six months earlier, he'd been promoted to lead a division of 200 people. The board celebrated. His team applauded. He felt ready.

Now he was texting me from his car in an empty parking lot, unable to go home and face his family. Unable to explain why success felt like failure. Unable to carry the weight one more day.

"I've delivered every number they asked for," he wrote. "But I've lost myself. My team is exhausted. My integrity feels compromised. I don't recognize who I'm becoming."

Over the next one hour or so, we talked. Not about strategy or performance metrics. About something more fundamental: what happens when leadership becomes disconnected from care.

He'd been trained in execution. He'd mastered frameworks. He knew how to drive results. But somewhere between the pressure to perform and the demand for speed, he'd lost the thread that holds leadership together: responsibility for the people entrusted to his care.

He wasn't alone.

The Crisis Nobody's Naming

I've spent decades working with leaders across business, technology, nonprofit, and faith-based organizations. I've watched brilliant people rise quickly, burn out quietly, and leave damage in their wake - not because they lacked skill, but because they lacked a grounded philosophy to guide everyday decisions.

The leadership culture we've created is loud, urgent, and relentless. It promises speed, scale, and success but offers little guidance on integrity, restraint, or stewardship. It celebrates visibility over responsibility. It rewards performance over character. It measures influence by numbers rather than by the lives strengthened or damaged along the way.
In those conditions, leadership becomes reactive. Decisions become transactional. Care becomes optional.

And leaders drift.

Not dramatically. Not suddenly. But slowly - one compromised decision at a time, one shortcut rationalized, one person overlooked in the rush to the next milestone.

I've watched leaders justify small ethical breaches because "everyone does it." I've seen them excuse poor treatment of people because "results matter most." I've witnessed them dismiss warning signs in their own behavior because "pressure is just part of leadership."

And I've watched the cost accumulate: broken trust, exhausted teams, fractured relationships, leaders who achieve everything and lose what matters most.

This playbook was written because we need a different orientation.

What This Playbook Offers

This is not another book promising quick results or easy answers. It offers something more durable: clarity, steadiness, and responsibility.

It is grounded in a simple but radical belief: leadership is not first about performance, but about responsibility. That authority is not ownership, but stewardship. That strength is not dominance, but discipline. And that care is not weakness, but the condition that keeps leadership from becoming reckless. The voices shaping leadership culture today are often disconnected from the weight leadership actually carries. They promise shortcuts. They celebrate hustle. They measure success by metrics that have nothing to do with the human cost of getting there.

Scripture has long provided a different compass - one that navigates power, influence, and responsibility with wisdom that doesn't shift with trends. Its insights are not abstract ideals. They are practical guidance for daily life, grounded in thousands of years of what actually works when leading people, managing resources, and stewarding influence.

In a world pulling leaders in many directions, this playbook draws from that wisdom to help leaders remain anchored.

Who This Is For

This playbook was written for leaders who are:

1. **Capable but exhausted** by transactional leadership culture
2. **Successful but unsettled** about who they're becoming
3. **Influential but uncertain** how to steward that influence responsibly
4. **Committed to excellence** without sacrificing character
5. **Navigating pressure** and need a grounded framework that holds

It's for the executive who delivers results but worries about the cost. The emerging leader who wants to build differently from the start. The ministry leader transitioning to marketplace influence. The manager who feels the weight of people depending on their decisions. The entrepreneur building something that will outlast the pressure of growth.

It's for anyone who suspects that leadership requires more than what the loud voices are offering.

What You'll Find Here

This book does not attempt to address every leadership challenge. Instead, it focuses on forming the kind of leader who can face those challenges with clarity, humility, and consistency.

It introduces a framework for how healthy leadership is built - not through quick fixes or performance hacks, but through the steady formation of character, responsibility, and care. Each of the ten principles builds on the previous one, creating a foundation that can sustain leadership through pressure, complexity, and change.

Each chapter provides:

- *A clear principle grounded in Scripture and experience*
- *Real-world examples from contemporary leaders*
- *Reflection practices you can apply immediately*
- *Wisdom that works regardless of your context*

This is not a book to rush through. It's designed to be used, revisited, and applied over time as your leadership seasons and responsibilities evolve.

A Word About What This Isn't

If you're looking for shortcuts, this book will frustrate you.

If you want tactics without character formation, you'll find this insufficient.

If you believe leadership is primarily about personal advancement, this will challenge that assumption.

But if you're looking for a grounded way to lead well-especially when the path is unclear, when pressure is constant, when values are tested - it was written for you.

The Leader I Told You About

That leader who texted me from the parking lot?
He didn't quit that night.

He took a two-week leave. He worked with a mentor. He got clear about what happened: he'd been put in an impossible position, forced to execute a mandate that violated everything he believed about leadership, and he'd complied without fighting for another way.

The exhaustion wasn't from working hard - it was from the moral weight of betraying people who trusted him. From executing layoffs he didn't believe in. From choosing compliance over conviction. From abandoning care because the cost of maintaining it felt too high.

He realized he had options he didn't take. He could have pushed back harder. He could have proposed alternatives. He could have been honest with his team about the pressure he was under instead of hiding. He could have executed the mandate with more humanity - communicating transparently, fighting for better severance, advocating for those being let go.

He couldn't change what the board demanded. But he could have changed how he carried it.

When he returned, he had hard conversations with his CEO about the culture this created, with his remaining team about what happened and why, with himself about the leader he wanted to be going forward. He set new boundaries. He rebuilt trust slowly, honestly. He recommitted to leading with care, even under pressure.

Eighteen months later, his division is stable. But more importantly, his team trusts him again. Turnover has dropped. People describe his leadership as "real" and "steady." He's navigated two more difficult decisions since then - but this time, with care at the center, not as an afterthought.
He still faces pressure. He still carries weight. But he's learned that success without care isn't success - it's just survival. And survival isn't what leadership is for.

Because he chose to rebuild with care.
You can too.

Lanre B. Olaleye

The Leadership with Care Framework

Leadership is not a collection of isolated traits.
It is a **progression of responsibilities that build on one another.**

The **Leadership with Care Framework** is a ten-part model that names how healthy leadership forms and matures over time. Each element corresponds to a chapter in this playbook and can be revisited as leadership seasons, pressures, and responsibilities change.

Rather than offering a checklist to master, this framework serves as a map - helping leaders understand where they are, what may be underdeveloped, and where attention is most needed.

The Arc of Leadership with Care

01

Care

Leadership begins with care. Care slows leaders down long enough to recognize the weight of their influence and the people entrusted to them. Without care, leadership becomes transactional and reckless.

02

Character

Care must be anchored in character. Character governs decisions when pressure increases and convenience tempts compromise. It keeps leadership steady when outcomes, incentives, or visibility create distortion.

03

Stewardship

Leadership is stewardship, not ownership. Stewards understand that authority, resources, and people are entrusted, not possessed and must be handled responsibly, humbly, and with an eye toward continuity beyond themselves.

04

Humility

Humility is strategic strength. It is power under discipline - authority exercised with restraint, openness to counsel, and a willingness to listen before acting.

05

Self-Leadership

Leaders must govern themselves before they can lead others. Emotional discipline, awareness, and regulation form the inner stability that sustains leadership under stress and keeps reactions from damaging trust.

06

Integrity

Integrity is consistency when no one is watching. It aligns private conduct with public responsibility and protects leadership credibility over time.

07

Words

Words shape culture. Leaders create environments through what they say, how they say it, and when they choose restraint-especially in digitally mediated, high-visibility settings.

08

Discipline

Discipline turns intention into reliability. Consistent habits, preparation, and follow-through allow leadership to endure beyond moments of talent or motivation.

09

Planning with Submission

Wise leaders plan diligently while holding outcomes humbly. Submission keeps planning flexible, responsive, and aligned with reality rather than ego, especially in fast changing, uncertain environments.

10

Justice, Fairness, and Trust

Leadership ultimately becomes visible through justice. Fair systems, consistent standards, and impartial decisions build trust-the lasting currency of influence for both people and the structures that support them.

How the Framework Is Meant to Be Used

This framework is not meant to be mastered quickly.

It is designed to:

Guide reflection over time

- *Shape daily leadership decisions*
- *Provide language for mentoring and coaching*
- *Anchor team conversations about how we lead, not just what we deliver*
- *Serve as a diagnostic when leadership feels strained or unclear*

Leaders may enter the framework at different points depending on season and responsibility. Over time, however, neglecting any one element will eventually strain the others.

Leaders may also use this framework with teams, mentors, or cohorts by choosing one element per month or quarter to focus on together, using the related chapter and practice as a shared reference point.

Leadership with care is not about perfection.

It is about alignment - bringing responsibility, character, and action into coherence.

A Question to Carry Forward

As you move into the chapters that follow, return often to this question:

Which part of this framework most needs attention in my leadership right now?

Growth begins where attention is honest.

The Leadership Self-Assessment at the end of this book mirrors this framework and is designed to help leaders reflect on how these elements are showing up in practice.

How to Use This Playbook

This is not a book to rush through.

It is a playbook designed to be used, revisited, and applied over time. You do not need to read it from beginning to end in one sitting. In fact, it will serve you best when engaged slowly and intentionally.

Read with Responsibility

Each chapter focuses on a single leadership principle. Read one chapter at a time, allowing space to reflect before moving on.

Leadership formation happens through:

- Thoughtful reading
- Honest reflection
- Repeated practice

This playbook is not about information accumulation. It is about ***leadership alignment.***

Engage the Practices

Every chapter includes a short leadership practice. These are not optional exercises - they are where the work happens.

Use the practices to:

- *Examine your current leadership posture*
- *Identify blind spots*
- *Strengthen habits that support long-term influence*

You do not need to complete every practice perfectly. You do need to approach them honestly.

Apply Before You Advance

Resist the urge to move on too quickly.

Leadership grows when insight is translated into action. After each chapter, ask:

- *What needs to change in how I lead?*
- *What decision, habit, or posture requires adjustment?*
- *Who is affected by this change?*

Apply one insight at a time. Small, consistent changes compound.

Use This in Community When Possible

Leadership is strengthened in community.
This playbook can be used:

- *Personally, for reflection and growth*
- *With a mentor, for guided discussion*
- *With a team, for leadership development*
- *In cohorts or workshops, for shared learning*

When discussed with others, prioritize listening over defending. Growth often comes through perspective.

Return to It Often

Leadership seasons change.
So will how this playbook speaks to you.

Revisit chapters when:

- *You face increased responsibility*
- *Pressure intensifies*
- *Decisions become complex*
- *Leadership feels heavy*

What you notice the second or third time may differ from what you noticed initially. That is part of the process.

A Final Word Before You Begin

This playbook does not promise quick results or easy leadership. It offers something more durable: clarity, steadiness, and responsibility.

Leadership is not perfected in moments.
It is practiced daily.

Begin with openness.
Proceed with discipline.
Lead with care.

Before You Begin

Leadership Diagnostic: **Where Are You Now?**

This brief assessment will help you identify which leadership areas need the most attention right now.

Leadership development isn't one-size-fits-all. You may be strong in some areas and struggling in others. This diagnostic helps you know where to focus as you read.

Instructions

Read each statement and rate yourself honestly based on your current behavior, not your intentions or aspirations.

Rating Scale:
1 = Rarely true / Significant struggle
2 = Sometimes true / Inconsistent
3 = Often true / Generally solid
4 = Consistently true / Clear strength

There are no right or wrong answers. This is about awareness, not judgment.

PART 1: Care & Responsibility

Statement 1: I regularly consider how my decisions affect the people under my influence before taking action.

☐ 1 - Rarely

☐ 2 - Sometimes

☐ 3 - Often

☐ 4 - Consistently

Statement 2: When making decisions under pressure, I slow down enough to weigh the impact on people, not just outcomes.

☐ 1 - Rarely

☐ 2 - Sometimes

☐ 3 - Often

☐ 4 - Consistently

Statement 3: I feel genuine responsibility for the wellbeing of the people I lead, not just their performance.

☐ 1 - Rarely

☐ 2 - Sometimes

☐ 3 - Often

☐ 4 - Consistently

Total Score (Part 1): ______ / 12

If you scored 6 or below, focus especially on Chapter 1: Care Is the First Responsibility

PART 2: Character & Integrity

Statement 4: My actions consistently align with my stated values, even when it's inconvenient.

☐ 1 - Rarely

☐ 2 - Sometimes

☐ 3 - Often

☐ 4 - Consistently

Statement 5: I hold myself to the same standards I expect of others-no exceptions.

☐ 1 - Rarely

☐ 2 - Sometimes

☐ 3 - Often

☐ 4 - Consistently

Statement 6: I maintain integrity in private (decisions, behavior, choices) even when no one is watching.

☐ 1 - Rarely

☐ 2 - Sometimes

☐ 3 - Often

☐ 4 - Consistently

Total Score (Part 2): ______ / 12

If you scored 6 or below, focus especially on **Chapter 2: Character Before Competence and Chapter 6: Integrity When No One Is Watching**

PART 3: Stewardship & Humility

Statement 7: I see my leadership role as stewardship (temporary responsibility) rather than ownership.

☐ 1 - Rarely

☐ 2 - Sometimes

☐ 3 - Often

☐ 4 - Consistently

Statement 8: I actively invite counsel and feedback before making major decisions.

☐ 1 - Rarely

☐ 2 - Sometimes

☐ 3 - Often

☐ 4 - Consistently

Statement 9: I delegate authority and trust others to make decisions without micromanaging.

☐ 1 - Rarely

☐ 2 - Sometimes

☐ 3 - Often

☐ 4 - Consistently

Total Score (Part3): ______ / 12

If you scored 6 or below, focus especially on **Chapter 3: Leadership Is Stewardship, Not Ownership and Chapter 4: Humility Is Strategic**

PART 4: Self-Leadership & Emotional Discipline

Statement 10: I govern my emotions rather than letting them govern me, especially under pressure.

☐ 1 - Rarely

☐ 2 - Sometimes

☐ 3 - Often

☐ 4 - Consistently

Statement 11: I pause before reacting when frustrated, angry, or anxious.

☐ 1 - Rarely

☐ 2 - Sometimes

☐ 3 - Often

☐ 4 - Consistently

Statement 12: I maintain composure and clarity during stressful or chaotic situations.

☐ 1 - Rarely

☐ 2 - Sometimes

☐ 3 - Often

☐ 4 - Consistently

Total Score (Part 4): ______ / 12

If you scored 6 or below, focus especially on **Chapter 5: Emotional Discipline and Self-Leadership**

PART 5: Words & Communication

Statement 13: My words generally bring clarity and calm rather than confusion or anxiety.

☐ 1 - Rarely

☐ 2 - Sometimes

☐ 3 - Often

☐ 4 - Consistently

Statement 14: I think carefully before speaking (or messaging digitally), especially when emotions are high.

☐ 1 - Rarely

☐ 2 - Sometimes

☐ 3 - Often

☐ 4 - Consistently

Statement 15: I correct privately and encourage publicly (not the reverse).

☐ 1 - Rarely

☐ 2 - Sometimes

☐ 3 - Often

☐ 4 - Consistently

Total Score (Part 5): _____ / 12

If you scored 6 or below, focus especially on **Chapter 7: Words Shape Culture**

PART 6: Discipline & Planning

Statement 16: I follow through on commitments consistently, not just when it's convenient.

☐ 1 - Rarely

☐ 2 - Sometimes

☐ 3 - Often

☐ 4 - Consistently

Statement 17: I prepare for my leadership responsibilities (meetings, decisions, conversations) rather than winging it.

☐ 1 - Rarely

☐ 2 - Sometimes

☐ 3 - Often

☐ 4 - Consistently

Statement 18: I plan strategically but hold plans flexibly-willing to adjust when circumstances change.

☐ 1 - Rarely

☐ 2 - Sometimes

☐ 3 - Often

☐ 4 - Consistently

Total Score (Part 6): ______ / 12

If you scored 6 or below, focus especially on **Chapter 8: Discipline Beats Talent and Chapter 9: Planning with Submission**

PART 7: Justice, Fairness & Trust

Statement 19: I apply standards consistently and fairly across all people and situations.

☐ 1 - Rarely
☐ 2 - Sometimes
☐ 3 - Often
☐ 4 - Consistently

Statement 20: People trust my decisions even when they disagree with them.

☐ 1 - Rarely
☐ 2 - Sometimes
☐ 3 - Often
☐ 4 - Consistently

Statement 21: I actively avoid favoritism and ensure everyone has equal access to opportunities.

☐ 1 - Rarely
☐ 2 - Sometimes
☐ 3 - Often
☐ 4 - Consistently

Total Score (Part 7): ______ / 12

If you scored 6 or below, focus especially on **Chapter 10: Justice, Fairness, and Trust**

YOUR DIAGNOSTIC RESULTS

Transfer your scores below:

Leadership Area	**Your Score**	**Chapter Focus**
Care & Responsibility	______ / **12**	Chapter 1
Character & Integrity	______ / **12**	Chapters 2, 6
Stewardship & Humility	______ / **12**	Chapters 3, 4
Self-Leadership & Emotional Discipline	______ / **12**	Chapter 5
Words & Communication	______ / **12**	Chapter 7
Discipline & Planning	______ / **12**	Chapters 8, 9
Justice, Fairness & Trust	______ / **12**	Chapter 10

INTERPRETING YOUR RESULTS

Scores of 9-12 (Strong Foundation)

This area is currently a leadership strength. As you read the corresponding chapter, focus on:

- Refining and deepening what you already do well
- Identifying how to help others develop in this area
- Staying vigilant against complacency

Scores of 6-8 (Developing Area)

This area is inconsistent-strong in some situations, weak in others. As you read the corresponding chapter, focus on:

- Understanding what triggers inconsistency
- Building systems and habits that create greater reliability
- Seeking accountability in this specific area

Scores of 3-5 (Growth Priority)

This area needs significant attention. As you read the corresponding chapter, focus on:

- Honest assessment of why this is a struggle
- Identifying 1-2 specific changes you can make immediately
- Finding a mentor or accountability partner to support growth

Scores of 0-2 (Urgent Development Need)

This area is currently a major gap in your leadership. As you read the corresponding chapter:

- Approach it as priority #1
- Consider working through it with a coach or mentor
- Return to this chapter multiple times
- Implement the practice exercises seriously

HOW TO USE THIS DIAGNOSTIC

Option 1: Read in Order, Focus on Weak Areas

Read the book from beginning to end, but spend extra time on chapters where you scored lowest. Complete all reflection exercises in those chapters.

Option 2: Start with Your Biggest Gap

If one area scored significantly lower than others, start with that chapter. Build momentum by addressing your most urgent development need first.

Option 3: Address All Areas Systematically

Work through the book one chapter at a time, completing all practices. Revisit this diagnostic every 3-6 months to track growth.

A NOTE BEFORE YOU BEGIN

Leadership development is not about perfection. It's about awareness, **honesty, and consistent growth.**

The fact that you're taking this diagnostic seriously shows you're already committed to growth. That commitment matters more than your current scores.

Low scores aren't failures-they're **invitations to growth.**
High scores aren't finish lines-they're **foundations to build on.**

Every leader has gaps. Every leader is growing. The question is: **Are you willing to see your gaps honestly and work on them intentionally?**

This book will help you do exactly that.

> ***Now, turn to Chapter 1 and begin the work of building leadership that sustains you and your people.***

Chapter One

Care Is the First Responsibility of Leadership

Leadership begins long before titles, influence, or recognition.
It begins with care.
Not sentiment.
Not good intentions.

But a deliberate concern for people, outcomes, and responsibility.

Anyone can occupy a role. Not everyone carries the weight of influence well. Leadership, at its core, is not about being in charge - it is about being responsible.

When people are affected by your decisions, your words, or your silence, you are leading whether you acknowledge it or not.

And that is where care becomes unavoidable.

Two Leaders, Two Outcomes

Let me share a story about two technology companies that faced the same crisis at the same time.

Company A: Leadership Without Care

In early 2020, a mid-sized software company faced sudden market disruption. Revenue projections collapsed overnight. The CEO called an emergency meeting with his executive team.

His approach was swift and decisive: immediate 20% workforce reduction, salary freezes for remaining staff, suspension of all non-essential benefits. The announcement was made via a company-wide email at 5 PM on a Friday. No warning. No conversation. No consideration for the lives impacted.

The email was cold, transactional, focused entirely on "organizational sustainability." It mentioned nothing about the people being let go - many of whom had been with the company for years, had relocated for their roles, had built their lives around the stability they'd been promised.

Within six months, the company lost not just those laid off, but 40% of the remaining workforce. Top performers left voluntarily. Clients began leaving, citing "instability" and "lack of trust." The company's Glassdoor rating plummeted. Recruiting became nearly impossible.

The CEO later defended his decisions in an industry interview: "I made the hard choices necessary for survival. Leadership requires toughness."

He was technically right about one thing: the cuts were necessary.

But the way they were executed destroyed something that took years to rebuild: trust.

Company B: Leadership With Care

A competitor faced identical market conditions. Same industry. Similar size. Same revenue collapse.

Their CEO also had to make difficult decisions. But her approach was different.

Before announcing anything, she:

- *Met personally with department heads to understand team situations*

- *Identified employees facing unique hardships (medical situations, family crises, recent relocations)*
- *Created a transition plan that included severance packages, extended healthcare, job placement support, and honest letters of recommendation*
- *Held town halls (virtual and in-person) to explain the situation transparently, answer questions, and acknowledge the pain*
- *Took a personal 40% salary cut before asking anyone else to sacrifice*

The announcement was made in a company meeting, not an email. She spoke honestly about the business reality, but also about the people affected. She cried during the meeting. Not performatively but genuinely. Because she cared about what this meant for people's lives.

The layoffs still happened. The cuts were still painful. But people felt ***seen***.

The results over the next 18 months:

- *Voluntary attrition among remaining staff: 8% (compared to 40% at Company A)*
- *Former employees spoke positively about the company publicly-some even returned when conditions improved*
- *Client retention remained strong because stability was maintained*
- *The company recovered faster and stronger*
- *Glassdoor rating improved*
- *Recruiting became easier because the company became known for "treating people right, even in hard times"*

Five years later, Company A is still struggling with trust issues and high turnover. Company B has tripled in size and is regularly named a "best place to work."

The difference wasn't the decisions made. It was how care shaped the way those decisions were carried out.

Care Is Not Soft- It Is Serious

In many environments, care is misunderstood. It is treated as weakness, emotionalism, or lack of firmness. But Scripture and experience teach otherwise.

Care is what forces a leader to:

- *Think before speaking*
- *Weigh decisions carefully*
- *Consider long-term impact over short-term convenience*
- *Act with restraint rather than impulse*

Care does not remove accountability. *It intensifies it.*

Leaders who do not care often lead recklessly. They may be decisive, but not discerning. They may be confident, but not wise. Eventually, the cost shows up in broken trust, exhausted people, and compromised outcomes.

Care slows a leader down just enough to ask better questions.

The Modern Care Crisis

We're living through what I call the ***"care recession"*** in leadership.

Research from Gallup (2023) shows:

- *Only 23% of employees worldwide feel their organization cares about their wellbeing*
- *76% of employees have experienced burnout in the past year*
- *The #1 reason people leave jobs is "feeling undervalued and uncared for"*

Yet leadership training still focuses primarily on strategy, execution, and performance metrics. Care is treated as a "soft skill" or relegated to HR responsibility.

This gap is costing organizations billions in turnover, lost productivity, and damaged reputation. More importantly, it's costing leaders their credibility and their teams their wellbeing.

The pandemic exposed this brutally. Leaders who genuinely cared about their people navigated uncertainty with trust intact. Leaders who didn't saw their teams fragment, disengage, or leave entirely.

Care became visible and so did its absence.

A Brief Illustration

A leader under pressure is asked to make a fast decision that will reduce costs but increase strain on a team already stretched thin. The data supports the move. The timeline demands speed.

Instead of acting immediately, the leader pauses long enough to gather input from those affected. The final decision still meets organizational goals, but it avoids unnecessary harm.

That pause was not indecision.
It was care at work.

Care does not always change decisions.
It often changes ***how decisions are made.***

Influence Without Care Is Dangerous

The higher your influence, the greater the consequence of neglect.

Every decision a leader makes creates a ripple:

- *A policy affects livelihoods*
- *A tone shapes culture*
- *A priority signals values*

When care is absent, people become expendable and results become everything. That is not leadership - that is management without conscience.

Scripture consistently connects leadership with responsibility toward others:

> *"Do nothing out of selfish ambition or vain conceit.*
> *Rather, in humility value others above yourselves,*

not looking to your own interests but each of you to the interests of the others."
- Philippians 2:3-4

This is not a call to weakness.
It is a call to mature leadership.

Care anchors leadership in humility. It reminds us that authority is not entitlement - it is stewardship.

Care Must Be Practiced, Not Claimed

Saying you care is easy.
Demonstrating care is costly.

Care shows up in:

- *How you listen*
- *How you correct*
- *How you plan*
- *How you respond under pressure*
- *How you treat people when outcomes are uncertain*

Care is revealed not in moments of comfort, but in moments of tension.

It shows when:

- *Feedback is uncomfortable*
- *Decisions are unpopular*
- *Results take time*
- *Pressure tempts shortcuts*

In my work with leaders across business, nonprofit, and faith-based settings, I have seen that leadership trouble rarely begins with moral collapse - it begins when care quietly gives way to convenience.

Leaders who care do not abdicate responsibility, but they also do not rush decisions that affect people's lives without thought.
Care disciplines leadership.

What Care Looks Like in Practice

Care is not abstract. It shows up in specific, observable behaviors:

In Communication:

- *You explain decisions, not just announce them*
- *You create space for questions and concerns*
- *You acknowledge the human impact of changes*
- *You listen to understand, not just to respond*

In Decision-Making:

- *You ask "Who will this affect?" before asking "What will this cost?"*
- *You gather input from those closest to the impact*
- *You consider second and third-order consequences*
- *You slow down when haste would cause harm*

In Crisis:

- *You prioritize people's dignity alongside organizational needs*
- *You over-communicate rather than under-communicate*
- *You acknowledge fear and uncertainty honestly*
- *You create support systems, not just survival plans*

In Daily Operations:

- *You notice when someone is struggling*
- *You check in, not just check off*
- *You celebrate growth, not just productivity*
- *You invest in development, not just deployment*

Care is not a program or a policy. It's a posture that shapes everything else.

The Cost of Leading with Care

Care-centered leadership is not convenient.

It requires:

- *Patience instead of haste*
- *Thoughtfulness instead of impulse*
- *Courage instead of indifference*

It means choosing clarity over control.

It means being willing to explain decisions, not just enforce them.
It means carrying the weight of outcomes instead of shifting blame.

But here is the truth:
Leadership without care eventually collapses under its own weight.

Care sustains leadership because it keeps leaders connected to purpose, to people, and to accountability.

When Company A's CEO was asked years later what he'd do differently, he said something revealing: "I'd probably make the same decisions. But I'd make them differently."

He'd learned too late that how matters as much as what. **Care determines the how.**

A Leadership Practice

Practice: Leadership Impact Audit

Before moving forward, pause and reflect honestly.

Ask yourself:

- *Who is affected by my leadership right now?*
- *How do my decisions shape their experience?*
- *Where might speed, pressure, or convenience be replacing care?*
- *What responsibility have I been given that I must steward more thoughtfully?*
- *If the people I lead were describing my leadership anonymously, what would they say about whether I care?*

Write it down.
Care becomes real when it becomes specific.

Additional Reflection: Think of a recent decision you made under pressure.

Walk through it again, slowly:

- Who was affected?
- Did you gather input from those closest to the impact?
- How was the decision communicated?
- What would have changed if care had been your primary filter?

Closing Reflection

Care is not the finish line of leadership - it is the starting point.

Before strategy.
Before execution.
Before outcomes.

If leadership is influence, then care determines whether that influence builds or damages, strengthens or erodes, multiplies or diminishes.

Every leader must answer this question - not once, but often:
Who am I carrying responsibility for, and how well am I caring for that responsibility?

The CEO of Company B still makes hard decisions. She still has difficult conversations. She still faces market pressure and organizational constraints.

But her people trust her. Because they know she cares.

And that trust has become her greatest strategic asset.

Care awakens responsibility.
Character determines whether that responsibility is carried consistently under pressure.

Do nothing out of selfish ambition or vain conceit. Rather, in humility value others above yourselves, not looking to your own interests but each of you to the interests of the others.

Philippians 2:3-4

Care establishes the ***foundation of leadership.***

But care without character becomes inconsistent when pressure increases. In the next chapter, we turn to character - the internal compass that keeps leadership steady when circumstances are uncertain and shortcuts are tempting.

Chapter Two
Character Before Competence

Competence attracts attention.
Character sustains leadership.

Many leaders rise because of what they can do. Far fewer remain effective because of who they are. Skills open doors, but character determines what happens once influence is gained.

This is why leadership failures are rarely about lack of ability. They are almost always about compromised judgment, unchecked ego, or erosion of integrity over time.

Competence can be learned.
Character must be formed.

The Temptation to Lead with Skill Alone

In fast-moving environments, competence is celebrated. Results matter. Execution matters. Performance matters.

But when competence becomes the primary measure of leadership, shortcuts follow.

Leaders begin to:

- *Justify small compromises for efficiency*
- *Excuse poor behavior because results are delivered*
- *Overlook warning signs in themselves and others*
- *Confuse effectiveness with trustworthiness*

The danger is subtle. Few leaders wake up intending to abandon integrity. Most drift-slowly-by prioritizing outcomes over principles.

Scripture is direct about this tension:

> *"The integrity of the upright guides them, but the unfaithful are destroyed by their duplicity."*
> ***- Proverbs 11:3***

Integrity does not simply protect reputation.
It guides decisions when pressure clouds judgment.

A Brief Illustration

A highly skilled leader delivers consistent results and is widely trusted because of performance. Over time, patterns emerge - dismissive comments, selective rule-bending, quiet exceptions made for convenience.

None of it seems severe enough to confront. The results are strong. The pressure is real.

Eventually, trust erodes - not because the leader lacked ability, but because people no longer trust the leader's judgment.

Character did not fail suddenly.
It was quietly displaced by convenience.

Character Is What Carries Weight Under Pressure

Leadership pressure exposes what training can't cover.

When stakes are high:

- *Policies won't save you*
- *Titles won't steady you*
- *Skill alone won't guide you*

Character becomes the internal compass.
It shapes:

- *How you handle power*
- *How you respond to temptation*
- *How you treat people who cannot benefit you*
- *How you decide when no option is ideal*

Leaders with strong character may still make difficult decisions, but they do so with restraint, fairness, and consistency. They are predictable in values, even when circumstances are unpredictable.

That consistency builds trust.

Why Integrity Is Leadership Currency

Trust is the currency of leadership, and integrity is how it is earned.
People do not expect perfection.
They expect consistency.

Integrity shows up when:

- *Words match actions*
- *Standards apply to everyone, including the leader*
- *Promises are kept, even when inconvenient*
- *Mistakes are acknowledged, not hidden*

Leaders who protect integrity protect the long-term health of the people and systems they lead.

Without integrity, competence becomes dangerous-because it enables influence without restraint.

The Quiet Erosion of Character

Character is rarely lost all at once.
It erodes quietly.

Often through:

- *Rationalizing small exceptions*
- *Ignoring internal discomfort*
- *Silencing corrective voices*
- *Allowing success to excuse behavior*

What begins as flexibility can become compromise.
What begins as confidence can harden into pride.

In my work with leaders across business, nonprofit, and faith-based settings, I have seen that the most damaging leadership failures rarely begin with scandal. They begin with **unchallenged drift** - when success shields leaders from necessary correction.

This is why character formation must be intentional. It does not grow automatically with experience. In fact, experience without reflection often entrenches poor habits.

Forming Character Deliberately

Character is formed through repeated choices, not grand gestures.

It is shaped by:

- *What you tolerate*
- *What you confront*
- *What you confess*
- *What you correct early*

Leaders serious about character create guardrails for themselves. They welcome accountability. They invite truth. They slow down when pressure tempts shortcuts.

They understand that leadership longevity depends more on who they are becoming than what they are achieving.

A Leadership Practice

Practice: Integrity Alignment Check

Ask yourself:

- *Where am I tempted to prioritize results over values?*
- *Are there standards I expect of others that I excuse in myself?*
- *What decision would I make if integrity-not convenience-were my guide?*
- *Who has permission to challenge my choices honestly?*

Be specific.
Character formation happens in real situations, not abstract ideals.

Closing Reflection

Competence will take you far.
Character will keep you steady.

Leadership is not sustained by talent alone, but by integrity that guides decisions when pressure is highest and visibility is lowest.

Every leader must decide-daily-what will lead them:
Skill, or character.

Those who choose character build leadership that lasts

The integrity of the upright guides them, but the unfaithful are destroyed by their duplicity.

Proverbs 11:3

*Character governs who a **leader is becoming.***

Stewardship governs how that character is expressed through authority, resources, and people entrusted to their care.

In the next chapter, we turn to leadership not as ownership-but as responsibility held on behalf of others.

Chapter Three

Leadership Is Stewardship, Not Ownership

One of the quickest ways leadership goes wrong is when authority is mistaken for ownership.

Titles, roles, and influence can create the illusion that people, outcomes, or organizations belong to the leader. But leadership was never meant to function that way.

Leaders do not own people.
They are entrusted with responsibility.

This distinction matters more than it seems. Ownership seeks control. Stewardship requires care, accountability, and faithfulness.

Two Founders, Two Exits

Let me show you what the difference between ownership and stewardship looks like when leaders face their greatest test: letting go.

Founder A: The Owner Who Couldn't Release

A tech startup founder built a successful company over 15 years. He was brilliant, visionary, and deeply committed. The company grew from his garage to 500 employees. Revenue hit $100 million. Investors were happy.

The board began discussing succession planning.

But the founder struggled. Every suggestion about transition was met with resistance. “Nobody understands this business like I do.” “I built this from nothing.” “They’ll ruin everything I created.”

When the board finally insisted on bringing in a COO to prepare for eventual transition, the founder:

- *Undermined the new hire in meetings*
- *Refused to delegate key decisions*
- *Created a shadow leadership structure loyal only to him*
- *Made critical decisions without consulting the executive team*
- *Sent late-night emails overriding decisions made during the day*

The message was clear: This is mine. I’m not letting go.

Within 18 months:

- *The COO resigned, citing “impossible working conditions”*
- *Three senior executives left*
- *Two board members resigned*
- *Company culture became toxic-people were afraid to make decisions*
- *Innovation stalled because nothing moved without the founder’s approval*
- *Growth plateaued*

The founder remained CEO, but the company he’d built began to slowly decay under the weight of his inability to release control. When later asked about succession, he said: “I gave my life to build this. Why should I hand it to someone who might destroy it?”

He saw the company as his possession. And possessions are protected, controlled, never released.

Founder B: The Steward Who Built for Transition

Another founder built a similar company - same industry, similar trajectory, comparable success. But when the board raised succession planning, his response was different:

"I've been preparing for this since day one."

He'd already been mentoring potential successors. He'd built systems that didn't depend on him. He'd encouraged leadership development at every level. He saw his role not as permanent owner, but as temporary steward.

His transition process:
Two years before stepping down, he identified and began mentoring his successor

- *He gradually transferred decision-making authority*
- *He remained available as advisor, not controller*
- *He celebrated the new CEO's early wins publicly*
- *He resisted the urge to intervene when decisions differed from what he would have done*
- *He trusted the board and the systems he'd built*

The result:

- *Seamless transition with zero executive turnover*
- *The new CEO brought fresh perspective that accelerated growth*
- *Company culture remained strong because trust was preserved*
- *The founder remained involved as board chair, but liberated from daily operations*
- *He was able to start new ventures and mentor other entrepreneurs*
- *Five years later, the company had tripled in value*

When asked about the transition, he said: "This was never mine to keep. I was stewarding it for a season. My job was to leave it stronger than I found it and ready for what comes next."

He saw leadership as a trust. And trusts are held temporarily, managed faithfully, and passed forward responsibly.

The difference? One leader confused authority with ownership. The other understood stewardship.

The Illusion of Ownership

When leaders act like owners, they begin to:

- *Guard power instead of sharing it*
- *Prioritize personal success over collective good*
- *Resist accountability*
- *Measure success by control rather than impact*

Ownership-centered leadership may achieve short-term results, but it often leaves damage in its wake - burnout, resentment, disengagement, and fear. Stewardship-centered leadership, by contrast, asks a different question: What has been entrusted to me, and how well am I caring for it?

Scripture frames leadership clearly:

> *"Now it is required that those who have been given a trust must prove faithful."*
> **- 1 Corinthians 4:1-2**

Faithfulness, not dominance, is the measure.

Why Ownership Thinking Destroys Leadership

The ownership mindset creates predictable problems:

1. It Makes Leaders Defensive

When you believe something belongs to you, any challenge feels like theft. Questions feel like attacks. Accountability feels like interference.

Owners resist:

- *Feedback ("You don't understand what I've built")*
- *Delegation ("Nobody will do it as well as I do")*
- *Transition ("This is mine, not theirs")*
- *Change ("Why fix what isn't broken?")*

This defensiveness creates isolation. Leaders surround themselves with people who agree, not people who strengthen.

2. It Creates Unhealthy Dependency

Ownership thinking centralizes power. Everything flows through the leader. Nothing moves without their approval.

This might feel like control, but it creates:

- *Bottlenecks*
- *Burnout (for the leader)*
- *Disengagement (for the team)*
- *Fragility (when the leader is absent)*

Organizations led by owners are only as strong as that one person. When they leave or fail, everything collapses.

3. It Prevents Growth

Owners don't develop successors - they see them as threats. They don't build systems - they become the system. They don't empower people - they control them.

This prevents:

- *Leadership development*
- *Innovation*
- *Sustainable growth*
- *Organizational maturity*

The company's ceiling becomes the leader's capacity.

4. It Damages People

Perhaps most dangerously, ownership thinking treats people as:

- *Resources to be consumed*
- *Means to an end*
- *Collateral damage for success*
- *Property to be managed*

When leaders own, people feel used rather than developed.

A Brief Illustration from Daily Leadership

A leader builds a team that performs well, but insists on being involved in every decision. Approvals bottleneck. Growth slows. People hesitate to take initiative without permission.

The leader believes this is diligence.
The team experiences it as control.

What was meant to protect outcomes begins to limit them.

Stewardship would have asked a different question - not "How do I stay in charge?" but *"How do I help others carry responsibility well?"*

Stewardship Reframes Authority

Stewardship does not weaken leadership.
It grounds it.

A steward understands that:

- *Influence is temporary*
- *Authority carries responsibility*
- *Power must be exercised with restraint*

This mindset changes how leaders approach decisions. They ask:

- *Who does this affect?*
- *What is the long-term impact?*
- *Am I acting for the good of those entrusted to me?*
- *How am I preparing this organization for when I'm no longer here?*

Stewardship produces leaders who are firm but fair, decisive but thoughtful, confident but accountable.

In my work with leaders across business, nonprofit, and faith-based settings, I have found that the healthiest leadership cultures are shaped not by how tightly authority is held, but by how responsibly it is shared.

People Are Not Tools

Perhaps the most important implication of stewardship is how leaders view people.

People are not:

- *Resources to be consumed*
- *Means to an end*
- *Collateral damage for success*

They are individuals entrusted to leadership care.
Stewardship insists that leaders:

- *Develop people, not just deploy them*
- *Protect dignity while pursuing excellence*
- *Correct behavior without diminishing worth*
- *Prepare successors, not protect positions*

Leaders who steward well leave people stronger, clearer, and more capable than they found them.

Ask yourself: Are the people I lead more empowered or more dependent because of my leadership?

The Weight of Responsibility

Stewardship acknowledges that leadership is weighty.
Leaders:

- *Shape culture*
- *Influence livelihoods*
- *Affect morale and direction*
- *Create environments where others either grow or shrink*

This weight should not intimidate leaders, but it should humble them. Stewardship invites leaders to carry responsibility with seriousness, not anxiety; with courage, not control.

The question is not "How long can I hold power?" but "How faithfully am I stewarding what's been entrusted?"

Modern Examples of Stewardship vs. Ownership

In Corporate Leadership

A global technology company's cultural transformation exemplifies stewardship:

- *The new CEO inherited an organization known for internal competition and control*
- *He shifted the culture from "know-it-all" to "learn-it-all"*
- *Empowered divisions to innovate independently*
- *Built systems designed to outlast his tenure*
- *Focused on long-term value creation over short-term control*

Contrast this with leaders who:

- *Stay decades past effectiveness to protect legacy*
- *Suppress innovation that threatens their vision*
- *Prevent leadership development to remain indispensable*

In Nonprofit Leadership

Strong nonprofit leaders:

- *Build boards that can govern without them*
- *Document processes so institutional knowledge transfers*
- *Celebrate when staff outgrow positions and move forward*
- *Measure success by mission impact, not personal visibility*

Weak nonprofit leaders:

- *Become the face and sole voice of the organization*
- *Create dependency on their fundraising relationships*
- *Leave vacuums when they depart because everything flowed through them*

In Ministry Leadership

- *Healthy church leaders:*
- *Develop multiple teachers and leaders*
- *Build systems for discipleship that don't require them*
- *Prepare the church for pastoral transition*
- *Measure success by mature disciples, not attendance at their services*

Unhealthy church leaders:

- *Build ministry around their personality*
- *Create cultures where they're the only voice that matters*
- *Resist raising up leaders who might "compete"*
- *Leave chaos when they transition because they built around themselves*

Letting Go Without Abdicating

Stewardship does not mean passivity. It means:

- *Delegating without disappearing*
- *Trusting without neglect*
- *Releasing control while maintaining accountability*

Healthy leaders know when to hold firm and when to step back. They resist the urge to micromanage, yet remain engaged. They understand that leadership success is not measured by how indispensable they are, but by how well others function.

The test of stewardship is this: If you stepped away tomorrow, would what you've built continue, grow, and thrive? Or would it collapse? If it would collapse, you've built dependency, not strength. You've owned, not stewarded.

A Leadership Practice

Practice: Stewardship Inventory

Reflect honestly:

1. **What responsibilities have been entrusted to me right now?**
   (List specific people, resources, outcomes, organizations)
2. **Where might I be acting like an owner instead of a steward?**

- Do I guard power or share it?
- Do I resist delegation?
- Do I see challenges as threats to my control?
- Do I measure success by my centrality?

3. **How am I caring for the people under my influence?**

- Are they growing or just performing?
- Are they empowered or dependent?
- Would they say I'm developing them or just using them?

4. **What would faithfulness look like in my current role?**

- What systems need to be built?
- What knowledge needs to be transferred?
- What leaders need to be developed?
- What would I need to do to prepare for my own irrelevance?

The Succession Test:

If you were told today you'd be transitioning out in 18 months, what would you need to do to ensure what you've built continues and thrives?

Write your responses.
Stewardship becomes clearer when responsibility is named.

Closing Reflection

Leadership is a trust.
It is not given to be possessed, but to be stewarded - wisely, humbly, and faithfully. When leaders shift from ownership to stewardship, leadership becomes less about control and more about care. Less about personal success and more about lasting impact.

That shift changes everything.
The founder who couldn't let go is still fighting to maintain control of a slowly declining organization. His inability to release has become the organization's greatest liability. The founder who stewarded is building his third company, mentoring dozens of leaders, and watching his first company thrive under new leadership.

One held tightly and lost influence.
One released faithfully and multiplied impact.

Which leader do you want to be?

This, then, is how you ought to regard us: as servants of Christ and as those entrusted with the mysteries God has revealed. Now it is required that those who have been given a trust must prove faithful."

1 Corinthians 4:1-2

If stewardship shapes how leaders hold authority, ***humility determines how that authority is exercised under pressure.***

In the next chapter, we turn to humility - not as weakness, but as strategic strength. Power under control.

Chapter Four

Humility Is Strategic

umility is often misunderstood in leadership.
It is mistaken for weakness, passivity, or lack of confidence. In reality, humility is one of the most strategic strengths a leader can possess.

Humility is not the absence of authority. It is authority exercised with restraint - **power under discipline.** Leaders who lack humility may appear strong, but they are often brittle. Leaders grounded in humility are resilient. They listen well, learn quickly, and adapt wisely.

Humility as Power Under Control

Every leader carries power-whether through position, expertise, influence, or access to resources.

Humility determines how that power is handled.

A humble leader:

- *Has authority, but does not dominate*
- *Has knowledge, but does not weaponize it*
- *Has influence, but does not intimidate*
- *Has confidence, but does not insist on being right*

This is not weakness.
It is strength governed by wisdom.

Uncontrolled power damages trust.
Controlled power builds it.

Why Humility Protects Leaders

Humility keeps leaders aligned with reality.

It reminds us that:

- *We do not see everything*
- *We do not know everything*
- *We benefit from perspective beyond our own*

Pride isolates. Humility invites input.
Scripture sets the foundation clearly:

> *"The fear of the LORD is the beginning of knowledge,*
> *but fools despise wisdom and instruction."*
> ***- Proverbs 1:7***

Leaders who submit their authority to wisdom are less likely to misuse it.

The Danger of Unsubmitted Leadership

Unsubmitted leaders often confuse confidence with infallibility.
They:

- *Resist feedback*
- *Dismiss counsel*
- *Interpret questions as challenges*
- *Surround themselves with agreement rather than truth*

Over time, blind spots form. Decisions narrow. Risk increases. Trust erodes. Humility keeps leaders teachable, not timid. It allows leaders to pause, listen, and reconsider-without losing authority.

Listening Is a Leadership Discipline

Humility expresses itself through listening.

Not performative listening.
Not waiting to respond.

But attentive listening that seeks understanding.
Listening does not slow leadership-it sharpens it.

Leaders who listen well:

- *Make better decisions*
- *Reduce unnecessary conflict*
- *Strengthen trust*
- *See around corners they would otherwise miss*

In moments of disagreement, humility may look as simple-and as difficult-as asking two clarifying questions before offering a position. That pause often reveals what certainty would have concealed.

Humility Does Not Remove Conviction

Humility does not mean indecision or lack of clarity.
A humble leader can still:

- *Set direction*
- *Enforce standards*
- *Make difficult calls*
- *Hold people accountable*

The difference is posture. Humble leaders do not lead to prove superiority. They lead to serve purpose.

They are firm without being harsh.
Clear without being arrogant.
Confident without being dismissive.

Learning as a Leadership Habit

Humility keeps leaders learning.

Experience is valuable-but when it replaces curiosity, growth stalls. Leaders who stop learning begin to rely on past success instead of present understanding. Humility sustains growth by keeping leaders open-to insight, correction, and refinement.

Leadership maturity is not a destination.
It is a discipline.

A Leadership Practice

Practice: Power and Posture Check

Ask yourself:

- *Where do I hold power in my leadership right now?*
- *How do I typically exercise that power-through control or restraint?*
- *When challenged, do I listen to understand or respond to defend?*
- *Where might humility strengthen my leadership effectiveness?*

Answer honestly.

Power becomes dangerous when posture is ignored.

Closing Reflection

Humility is not optional for leadership longevity.

It is power under control.
Strength under discipline.
Authority governed by wisdom.

Leaders who cultivate humility do not lose influence-they gain credibility. In a world that rewards noise and dominance, humility remains one of the most strategic leadership advantages available.

The fear of the LORD is the beginning of knowledge, but fools despise wisdom and instruction.

Proverbs 1:7

If humility governs how leaders hold power, ***the next challenge is how they manage themselves under pressure.***

In the next chapter, we turn inward to emotional discipline and self-leadership - the inner work that prevents external authority from becoming destructive.

Chapter Five

Emotional Discipline and Self-Leadership

Before leaders manage teams, projects, or outcomes, they are managing themselves.

This is where leadership often succeeds-or quietly unravels.
Emotional discipline is not about suppressing feelings or pretending pressure does not exist. It is about governing responses, especially when emotions are strong and circumstances are demanding.

Leadership does not remove emotion.
It requires mastery over it.

Why Self-Leadership Comes First

Every leader brings their emotional state into the room, whether intentionally or not.

Anxious leaders create anxious environments.
Reactive leaders create unstable cultures.
Centered leaders create clarity.

Self-leadership is the ability to:

- *Pause before reacting*
- *Respond instead of retaliating*
- *Choose clarity over impulse*
- *Maintain composure under pressure*

Scripture captures this principle plainly:

"Better a patient person than a warrior,
one with self-control than one who takes a city."
- Proverbs 16:32

In leadership, self-control is strength.

Emotional Discipline Is Not Emotional Absence

Emotion is not the enemy. Unexamined emotion is.
Leaders feel:

- *Frustration when progress stalls*
- *Anger when standards are ignored*
- *Fear when outcomes are uncertain*
- *Disappointment when expectations are unmet*

Emotional discipline does not deny these realities. It acknowledges them-then refuses to let them drive decisions unchecked.

Unregulated emotion often shows up as:

- *Sharp words spoken too quickly*
- *Defensive reactions to feedback*
- *Impulsive decisions later regretted*
- *Silent withdrawal instead of engagement*

Self-leadership interrupts these patterns.

Pressure Reveals Emotional Habits

Leadership pressure does not create emotional habits-it reveals them.
Under stress, leaders default to what they have practiced:

- *Some tighten control*
- *Some raise their voice*
- *Some avoid difficult conversations*
- *Some disengage emotionally*

Emotional discipline is built before pressure arrives.
It is formed through:

- *Reflection*
- *Awareness*
- *Repeated restraint*
- *Intentional response*

Leaders who cultivate emotional discipline are less reactive and more reliable. In my work with leaders navigating high-stakes decisions, I have seen that the most trusted leaders are not those who feel the least-but those who regulate the most.

Breaking the Cycle: Why Leaders Become What They Hated

There's a disturbing pattern in leadership that plays out repeatedly:

The employee who complained bitterly about their micromanaging boss becomes a micromanager the moment they're promoted.

The team member who resented being yelled at in meetings starts yelling at their own team.

The professional who criticized their manager for never listening becomes the manager who doesn't listen.

People become exactly what they hated-sometimes worse.

This isn't hypocrisy. It's unexamined emotional patterns reproducing themselves under pressure.

Here's what happens:

When you're managed poorly, you experience pain. Frustration. Resentment. Powerlessness. You tell yourself: "When I'm in charge, I'll never do this to people."

But you never process the wound. You never examine why that behavior hurt. You never develop alternative responses. You never do the inner work to understand what drove your manager's behavior-and what might drive yours.

Then you get promoted. Suddenly you face the same pressures your manager faced: tight deadlines, demanding executives, resource constraints, accountability for outcomes you can't fully control.

And you default to what you know. Not to what you believe, but to what you experienced. The neural pathways are already there. The behaviors are familiar. Under stress, you reach for the management style that's been modeled for you-even if you hated it.

Micromanaging feels like diligence. "I'm just making sure things get done right."

Yelling feels like urgency. "People need to understand how serious this is."

Not listening feels like efficiency. "I don't have time for endless discussion."

You rationalize the exact behaviors you once condemned.

Breaking this cycle requires self-leadership.

It requires:

1. Recognizing the pattern before you're in power

While you're still being managed, ask yourself: "What is this teaching me about how NOT to lead? What alternative would I model if I had the chance?"

Write it down. Be specific. Don't just say "I won't micromanage"-describe what healthy delegation actually looks like.

2. Examining why the behavior hurt

What made your manager's approach damaging? Was it:

- *Lack of trust?*
- *Disrespect for your judgment?*
- *Failure to explain the "why"?*
- *Creating fear instead of clarity?*

Understanding the why helps you avoid reproducing the harm.

3. Developing alternative responses before pressure hits

Don't wait until you're a manager to decide how you'll manage. Practice now:

- When you see poor leadership, identify what the better alternative would be
- When you experience frustration with authority, notice your emotional response - that's the pattern you'll need to interrupt later
- Build habits of patience, listening, and restraint before you have power

4. Getting accountability when you step into leadership

When you become a manager, tell your team: "I've experienced poor management. I don't want to reproduce it. If you see me slipping into patterns that damage trust or respect, please tell me."

Make it safe for people to give you feedback. Otherwise, you won't see yourself drifting.

5. Pausing when you feel the urge to react as you were managed

When you catch yourself about to micromanage, yell, or dismiss someone's

input-pause.
Ask: "Is this how I wanted to be led? Or is this the wounded pattern reproducing itself?"

That pause is where self-leadership happens.

The cycle breaks when leaders do the inner work.
You don't automatically become a good manager just because you experienced bad management. You become a good manager when you:

- *Examine the wounds*
- *Identify the patterns*
- *Develop alternatives*
- *Practice emotional discipline*
- *Invite accountability*

Otherwise, you'll reproduce exactly what you hated and wonder why your team resents you the way you once resented your boss.

Self-leadership is how you become the leader you needed when you were the one being led.

The Power of the Pause

One of the most underrated leadership skills is the ability to pause.
A pause:

- *Creates space between stimulus and response*
- *Prevents unnecessary damage*
- *Allows wisdom to catch up with emotion*

Pausing is not avoidance. It is leadership restraint.
Leaders who pause:

- *Ask better questions*
- *Speak with greater precision*
- *Preserve trust during conflict*
- *Reduce regret after decisions*

The pause protects both people and outcomes.

Emotional Discipline Builds Trust

People watch how leaders handle pressure.

They notice:

- *Tone in difficult conversations*
- *Consistency under stress*
- *Fairness when emotions run high*
- *Stability during uncertainty*

Leaders who govern their emotions well become predictable in the best way. Their teams know what to expect-even in hard moments.

That predictability builds trust.

For some leaders, developing this discipline may require intentional support-coaching, mentorship, spiritual direction, or trusted accountability. Seeking help is not weakness; it is wisdom.

A Leadership Practice

Practice: Emotional Awareness Check

Reflect honestly:

- *What situations most easily trigger my emotions?*
- *How do I typically respond under pressure?*
- *What words or behaviors do I regret after stressful moments?*
- *What would restraint look like in my current leadership context?*

Choose one upcoming situation where you will intentionally pause before responding. Self-leadership grows through practice, not intention alone.

Closing Reflection

Leadership strength is not measured by emotional force, but by emotional discipline. Those who lead themselves well create space for others to perform, grow, and trust. They bring steadiness where chaos might otherwise spread.

Before you can regulate an organization, you must learn to regulate yourself. That work is quiet. But its impact is lasting.

Better a patient person than a warrior, one with self-control than one who takes a city

Proverbs 16:32

If emotional discipline governs how leaders respond under pressure, ***integrity determines how they act when no one is watching.***

In the next chapter, we turn to private consistency - the unseen choices that ultimately shape public credibility.

Chapter Six

Integrity When No One Is Watching

Much of leadership happens in public.
But integrity is formed in private.

What leaders do when observed matters. What they do when no one is watching matters more. Integrity is not situational. It does not shift with visibility, convenience, or pressure. It is the internal alignment between values and actions, especially when shortcuts are available and accountability feels distant.

Leadership credibility is built quietly, long before it is tested publicly.

The Private Life of Leadership

Every leader has two environments:

- The visible environment, where decisions are seen and evaluated
- The private environment, where motives, habits, and choices are hidden

The private environment shapes the public one.

Private compromises rarely stay private. They eventually surface as:

- *Inconsistent decisions*
- *Eroded trust*
- *Ethical blind spots*
- *Rationalized behavior*

Scripture speaks directly to this reality:

"Whoever walks in integrity walks securely,
but whoever takes crooked paths will be found out."
- Proverbs 10:9

Integrity is not just moral alignment-it is leadership security.

Integrity Is Consistency, Not Perfection Integrity does not mean leaders never make mistakes. It means they respond to mistakes honestly.

Leaders with integrity:

- *Admit errors rather than conceal them*
- *Correct missteps rather than justify them*
- *Accept responsibility rather than deflect blame*

People are not looking for flawless leaders.
They are looking for trustworthy ones.

Consistency builds credibility.
Inconsistency erodes it.

The Quiet Temptations Leaders Face

Integrity is most tested not in dramatic moments, but in subtle ones.
Small choices such as:

- *Bending standards "just this once"*
- *Withholding truth to avoid discomfort*
- *Using authority for personal convenience*
- *Ignoring issues that require difficult conversations*

These moments feel minor-but they shape leadership character. Unchecked, small compromises accumulate. Over time, leaders begin to normalize behavior they once would have questioned.

It is often in private emails, informal conversations, expense decisions, or unseen approvals that integrity is most quietly tested.
Integrity requires vigilance.

Why Integrity Protects Everyone

When leaders lack integrity, the cost is never personal alone.
It affects:

- *Team morale*
- *Organizational culture*
- *Decision quality*
- *Long-term sustainability*

Conversely, leaders who model integrity create environments where:

- *Trust is safe*
- *Standards are clear*
- *Accountability is fair*
- *People feel secure*

Integrity stabilizes leadership systems. It reduces fear and increases confidence. In my experience, teams are far more willing to endure difficult seasons under leaders they trust than to thrive briefly under leaders they doubt.

Choosing Integrity Under Pressure

Pressure does not eliminate integrity-it reveals priorities.
Leaders who choose integrity under pressure:

- *Speak truth when silence is easier*
- *Act fairly when favoritism is tempting*
- *Uphold standards when shortcuts promise speed*

These choices are rarely applauded in the moment.
But they compound over time.

Integrity builds leadership capital that cannot be manufactured.

A Leadership Practice

Practice: Integrity Audit

Ask yourself honestly:

- *Where am I most tempted to compromise privately?*
- *Are there standards I enforce publicly but relax personally?*
- *What decisions would I change if they were made visible?*
- *Who holds me accountable when no one else can?*

Write your answers.
Integrity strengthens when it is examined.

Closing Reflection

Leadership is tested in moments no one documents and few applaud. Integrity formed in private determines credibility sustained in public. Leaders who guard integrity when unseen build leadership that endures scrutiny when exposed.

What you tolerate privately eventually shapes what you allow publicly.
Choose integrity-especially when no one is watching.

Whoever walks in integrity walks securely, but whoever takes crooked paths will be found out.

Proverbs 10:9

If integrity governs what leaders do in private, ***words reveal what leaders value in public.***

In the next chapter, we turn to language - how words shape culture, trust, and direction far more than leaders often realize.

Chapter Seven

Words Shape Culture

Every leader creates culture - whether intentionally or not. And one of the most powerful tools shaping that culture is speech.

Words are not neutral. They carry weight. They set tone. They signal what matters and what does not. Long before policies take root, language does. Leaders often underestimate how closely people listen - not only to what they say, but to how they say it.

The Slack Message That Changed Everything

A mid-sized marketing agency had built a reputation for creativity and collaboration. The culture was strong. Retention was high. Clients loved working with them.

Then came the message.

It was 9:47 PM on a Tuesday. The CEO, frustrated by a project delay, sent a message in the company's main Slack channel:

> *"Seriously? Another missed deadline? I'm starting to wonder if anyone here actually cares about quality. This is embarrassing."*

The message sat there. Visible to all 85 employees. No context. No private conversation first. Just public frustration, vented downward.

Within hours:

- *The project lead (who'd been working 60-hour weeks and dealing with a family medical crisis) submitted his resignation*
- *Three team members posted their resumes on LinkedIn*
- *The company Slack went silent- people stopped communicating openly, afraid anything they said might trigger another outburst*
- *Morale collapsed overnight*

The CEO later tried to walk it back. "I was just frustrated. People are too sensitive. It wasn't that serious."

But the damage was done.

Here's what that one message communicated:

- Mistakes will be publicly shamed
- Context doesn't matter
- Your leader's emotional state is more important than your wellbeing
- This workspace is not safe

Six months later:

- 20% of the team had left
- Client projects suffered due to instability
- The culture of openness was replaced by fear and caution
- Recruiting became difficult as word spread

One message. Nine sentences. Irreversible damage.

The Digital Amplification Effect

We're living through a revolution in workplace communication and most leaders haven't adapted their speech habits to match.

Twenty years ago, a leader's careless comment in a hallway conversation affected maybe 2-3 people. Today, that same comment:

- Posted in Slack reaches 500 people instantly
- Forwarded in WhatsApp spreads to clients and competitors
- Screenshot and shared on Twitter becomes permanent
- Discussed in private channels you'll never see

Digital communication amplifies everything:

- Speed (instant)
- Reach (everyone, simultaneously)
- Permanence (screenshots live forever)
- Interpretation (no tone, no body language, no context)

And yet many leaders still communicate digitally the way they used to communicate verbally - casually, impulsively, without considering the reach or permanence of their words.

This is creating a leadership communication crisis.

The Modern Word Crisis: By the Numbers

Recent research reveals the scope:

Slack/Teams Data (2023-2024):

- 67% of employees report seeing messages from leadership that "shouldn't have been sent"
- 43% have witnessed a leader publicly criticize someone in a digital channel
- 52% say they've seen tone-deaf messages from leadership during crises
- 78% report feeling anxious when they see a notification from leadership after hours

Email Statistics:

- The average knowledge worker receives 120 emails per day
- 62% of workplace emails contain tone that's misinterpreted
- 31% of workplace conflict originates from email miscommunication
- Leaders send 3x more after-hours emails than they realize

The Cost:

- $62 billion annually lost to communication failures in US businesses alone
- 86% of employees cite "lack of effective communication" as a primary workplace problem
- Poor communication is the #2 reason talented people leave organizations

Your words - especially in digital form, are shaping culture more powerfully than you realize.

Speech as a Leadership Instrument

Leadership speech does more than convey information. It:

- Frames priorities
- Clarifies expectations
- Reinforces values
- Builds or erodes trust

The same message can inspire confidence or create anxiety depending on delivery.

Scripture captures the gravity of words succinctly:

"The tongue has the power of life and death."

- Proverbs 18:21

For leaders, this is not poetic language.
It is practical wisdom.

And in the digital age, the "tongue" includes:

- Email
- Slack/Teams messages
- Text messages
- WhatsApp/Signal
- Video calls
- Voice memos
- Social media posts

Every platform amplifies your words. Every channel extends your reach. Every message you send is shaping culture - for better or worse.

Tone Communicates Before Content

People hear tone before they process meaning.

A leader's tone can:

- *De-escalate tension*
- *Intensify conflict*
- *Invite dialogue*
- *Shut it down completely*

Leaders who speak harshly may deliver truth, but often lose trust. Leaders who avoid clarity may preserve comfort, but sacrifice direction.

Effective leadership speech balances:

- Clarity without cruelty
- Honesty without humiliation
- Authority without intimidation

Tone is not an accessory to leadership.
It is part of the message.

And in digital communication, tone is even harder to control and easier to misread.

Consider:

In-person: *"We need to talk about the project timeline."*

(Can be softened with facial expression, tone of voice, immediate clarification)

Via Slack: *"We need to talk about the project timeline."*

(Reads as threatening. No softening cues. Person spends next hour anxious.)

The words are identical. The impact is vastly different.

Words in Moments of Pressure

Pressure reveals speech habits.

Under stress, leaders may:

- Speak too quickly
- Speak too sharply
- Say more than necessary

- Say less than required

Words spoken in pressure linger longer than words spoken in ease.
A careless comment can undermine months of trust. A thoughtful word can steady an entire team.
This is why disciplined leaders are intentional with speech, especially when emotions are elevated.

In digital environments - emails, chats, Slack threads, WhatsApp messages-tone is even easier to misread, and careless words travel faster and farther than intended.

The 24-Hour Rule for Digital Communication Under Pressure

When you're frustrated, angry, or anxious:

1. *Write the message if you need to process*
2. *Save it as a draft*
3. *Wait 24 hours (or at minimum, 2 hours)*
4. *Reread before sending*
5. Ask: "If this were screenshot and shared publicly, would I be proud of it?"

If the answer is no, rewrite it. Or pick up the phone instead.

The Three Categories of Leadership Speech

Leadership speech generally falls into three categories:

1. Correction

Necessary, but dangerous when done carelessly.

Poor Digital Correction:

"This report is unacceptable. Redo it."
(Sent via email at 10 PM, CC'ing the entire team)

Effect: Humiliation, defensiveness, fear

Better Correction:

"Let's schedule 15 minutes tomorrow to discuss the report. I have some feedback that will help strengthen it."

(Sent privately, during work hours, with specific time commitment)

Effect: Dignity preserved, problem addressed, trust maintained

Rule: Correct privately when possible. Never publicly humiliate digitally.

2. Encouragement

Underutilized, especially in digital channels.

Leaders tend to:

- Quickly point out problems (via Slack/email)
- Slowly acknowledge wins (if at all)

This imbalance creates cultures where people only hear from leadership when something's wrong.

Best Practice:

- Make encouragement public (channel-wide recognition)
- Make correction private (DM or in-person)
- Send 3x more encouraging messages than corrective ones

3. Restraint

Sometimes the most powerful leadership speech is ***silence.***

Not every thought needs to be expressed.

Not every frustration needs to be shared.

Not every opinion needs to be posted.

Leaders who lack restraint:

- Vent in team channels (creating anxiety)
- Share frustrations about senior leadership with direct reports (undermining trust)
- Post impulsively on company Slack (creating confusion)
- Send stream-of-consciousness emails at 2 AM (creating chaos)

Leaders who practice restraint:

- Process emotions privately or with appropriate peers

- Speak only when they have something constructive to add
- Consider whether the message will help or harm before sending

Ask before hitting send: "Does this message make things better or just make me feel better?"

The Danger of Venting Downward

One of the most damaging leadership habits is venting downward - expressing frustration to those who lack power to respond.

This often looks like a leader unloading complaints about senior leadership, organizational constraints, or unresolved conflict to direct reports.

Example:
A manager, frustrated with a decision from the C-suite, messages their team:

> *"Well, corporate has made another brilliant decision that makes no sense. Guess we'll just have to deal with it. Classic."*

What the manager thinks they're communicating:

- Transparency
- Solidarity with the team
- Honesty about constraints

What the team actually hears:

- Our leader doesn't support leadership
- This organization is dysfunctional
- We're powerless
- There's no point in trying

It creates:

- Fear instead of trust
- Anxiety instead of clarity
- Compliance instead of commitment

Leaders need spaces to process emotion but those spaces should be appropriate, not positional.

Process with:

- *Peers*
- *Mentors*
- *Coaches*
- *Appropriate senior leaders*

Don't process with:

- *Direct reports*
- *Public channels*
- *Subordinates who can't challenge you*

Self-control in speech protects people who cannot protect themselves.

Digital Communication Best Practices for Leaders

Email Discipline

Do:

- Use email for information, documentation, and formal communication
- Be concise and clear
- Assume it will be forwarded
- Send during work hours when possible
- Use subject lines that clarify urgency and topic

Don't:

- Send emotional emails immediately
- Use email for complex, nuanced conversations
- CC people to create public pressure
- Send after-hours unless truly urgent
- Use ALL CAPS or excessive punctuation (!!!)

Slack/Teams Discipline

Do:

- Use for quick coordination and updates
- Encourage open dialogue
- Model healthy boundaries (don't message at midnight)
- Acknowledge good work publicly
- Use threads to keep conversations organized

Don't:

- Publicly correct or criticize
- Send vague messages that create anxiety ("We need to talk")
- Expect immediate responses
- Create FOMO by having important conversations in private channels
- Let your mood dictate your messages

Text/WhatsApp Discipline

Do:

- Use for time-sensitive coordination
- Keep it brief
- Respect off-hours boundaries
- Be extra clear (no room for misinterpretation)

Don't:

- Use for serious conversations
- Send bad news via text
- Create group chats that exclude some team members
- Text when a call would be clearer
- Assume tone will translate

Video Call Discipline

Do:

- Turn your camera on when possible (builds connection)
- Eliminate distractions
- Give people full attention
- Mute when not speaking
- Follow up with written summary

Don't:

- Multitask visibly
- Take calls from distracting locations
- Interrupt
- Forget you're on camera

When to Move From Digital to Direct

Some conversations should never happen digitally:

Always move to phone/video/in-person for:

- Performance issues
- Conflict resolution
- Sensitive feedback
- Layoffs or terminations
- Major organizational changes
- Emotional or personal topics
- Anything where tone matters significantly

Red Flag Test: If you're worried about how a message might be received, don't send it digitally. Pick up the phone.

A Leadership Practice

Practice: Speech Awareness Audit

Reflect honestly:

1. Digital Communication Patterns:

- Review your last 20 messages in Slack/Teams/email
- What tone comes through?
- How often do you correct vs. encourage?
- When do you send messages (work hours vs. off-hours)?
- Would you be proud if any of these were screenshot and shared?

2. Under Pressure Assessment:

- When under pressure, do my words calm or intensify situations?
- Do I vent frustration in team channels?
- Do I send impulsive messages I later regret?
- Where might silence serve better than immediate response?

3. Recipient Perspective:

How do people likely feel after digital conversations with me?
Do my messages create clarity or anxiety?
Am I over-communicating or under-communicating?
Do people feel safe bringing me problems, or afraid of my reaction?

4. This Week's Commitment:

Choose one upcoming conversation where you will speak more intentionally than usual.
Specifically:

- If it's sensitive, have it in person or by phone (not email/Slack)
- If you're frustrated, wait 24 hours before sending
- If it's correction, do it privately
- If it's encouragement, do it publicly

Additional Exercise: The Screenshot Test

Before sending any message, ask:

> *"If this were screenshot and sent to the person I respect most, would I be proud of it?"*

If no, rewrite or don't send.

Closing Reflection

Leaders speak culture into existence.
Over time, language becomes atmosphere and atmosphere becomes expectation.
Every word you choose contributes to the environment people work, grow, and lead within. In a digital age where words travel instantly, reach everyone simultaneously, and live forever in screenshots, your communication discipline has never mattered more.

The CEO who sent that Slack message learned this the hard way. Years later, when asked what he'd do differently, he said:

"I'd pick up the phone. Or better yet, I'd wait until morning, calm down, and then have a real conversation. That one message cost me incredible people, damaged relationships I'd built over years, and taught me that leadership speech isn't just about what you say - it's about how, when, where, and whether you say it at all."

Choose words that clarify, strengthen, and stabilize.
Especially in the digital spaces where most leadership communication now happens.

The tongue has the power of life and death, and those who love it will eat its fruit.

Proverbs 18:21

If words shape culture in moments, ***discipline sustains culture over time.***

In the next chapter, we turn to discipline, not talent as the quiet force that determines whether leadership endures or burns out.

Chapter Eight

Discipline Beats Talent

Talent gets attention.

Discipline gets results.

Many leaders rise because they are gifted. Far fewer sustain influence because they are consistent. Talent may impress, but discipline quietly compounds over time.

Leadership effectiveness is rarely determined by brilliance in moments. It is determined by what a leader does repeatedly.

Why Talent Is Overrated

Talent can mask weaknesses - at least for a while.

Gifted leaders may:

- *Rely on instinct instead of preparation*
- *Win early without building systems*
- *Succeed despite habits rather than because of them*

But talent without discipline is fragile. When pressure increases or complexity grows, raw ability alone begins to fail.

Scripture offers a simple contrast:

"Lazy hands make for poverty,
but diligent hands bring wealth."

- Proverbs 10:4

The emphasis is not intelligence or creativity.
It is diligence.

Discipline Is Leadership Reliability

Discipline makes leadership reliable.
It shows up in:

- Preparation before meetings
- Follow-through after decisions
- Consistency in standards
- Faithfulness in small responsibilities

People trust leaders who are disciplined because they know what to expect. There is stability in predictability. Discipline turns leadership from occasional excellence into sustained effectiveness. Disciplined leaders pace themselves. Undisciplined leaders often burn out themselves and those around them.

Habits Shape Outcomes

Leaders do not drift into excellence.
They drift into inconsistency.

Outcomes reflect habits:

- Clear leaders build clarity through preparation
- Calm leaders cultivate calm through restraint
- Effective leaders execute because they practice follow-through

Discipline is not dramatic. It is often unseen. But it quietly shapes culture and performance. What leaders practice becomes what organizations normalize.

Modeling Before Demanding

One of the fastest ways to undermine leadership credibility is to demand discipline from others without practicing it personally.
Leaders set expectations not only through instruction, but through example.

Disciplined leaders:

- Arrive prepared
- Honor time commitments
- Follow up on commitments made
- Maintain standards consistently

This modeling creates permission for others to do the same.
Discipline earns moral authority.

In my experience, teams will tolerate imperfect systems far longer than they will tolerate inconsistent leadership.

Discipline Is a Choice Repeated Daily

Discipline is not personality-based.
It is decision-based.
It does not require motivation.
It requires commitment.

Leaders who rely on motivation struggle with consistency. Leaders who rely on discipline build momentum - even when motivation fades.
Small, repeated choices accumulate into leadership strength.

A Leadership Practice

Practice: Discipline Inventory

Ask yourself:

- Where does inconsistency show up most in my leadership?
- What small habit would most improve my effectiveness?
- Where am I relying on talent instead of preparation?
- What discipline, if practiced daily, would compound over time?

Choose one habit to strengthen this week.
Leadership growth accelerates through focus, not overload.

Closing Reflection

Talent may open doors, but discipline keeps them open.

Leadership is not sustained by flashes of brilliance, but by steady commitment to doing the right things consistently.

Those who lead well over time are not always the most gifted but they are almost always the most disciplined.

Lazy hands make for poverty, but diligent hands bring wealth.

Proverbs 10:4

Discipline shapes how leaders work daily. ***Planning shapes where that work is directed***

In the next chapter, we turn to planning, not as control, but as submission - how leaders plan seriously while holding outcomes wisely.

Chapter Nine

Planning with Submission

Good leaders plan.
Wise leaders plan with submission.

Planning is not optional in leadership. Vision without structure is wishful thinking. Direction without preparation creates confusion. Leaders are expected to think ahead, anticipate challenges, and set a course. Yet planning becomes dangerous when it hardens into control.
Submission keeps planning honest.

The Tension Every Leader Must Manage

Leaders live in tension:

- *Responsibility to plan*
- *Humility to submit outcomes*

Planning asserts intent.
Submission acknowledges limitation.

Leaders who ignore planning drift.
Leaders who ignore submission overreach.

Scripture holds both together:

"Commit to the LORD whatever you do,
and he will establish your plans."
- Proverbs 16:3

The call is not to abandon planning, but to anchor it.

Planning Without Submission Breeds Arrogance

When leaders plan without submission, they:

- Overestimate their control
- Dismiss warning signs
- Resist course correction
- Interpret obstacles as threats rather than signals

Unsubmitted planning often shows up as rigidity. Leaders cling to plans even when circumstances change, people are harmed, or new information emerges.

Planning becomes an identity rather than a tool. Submission restores flexibility.

Submission Is Not Passivity

Submission does not mean indecision, delay, or lack of confidence.
Submitted leaders still:

- *Set goals*
- *Make timelines*
- *Allocate resources*
- *Hold people accountable*

The difference is posture.
Submitted leaders plan seriously but remain willing to:

- *Revisit assumptions*
- *Adjust direction*
- *Admit misjudgment*
- *Release outcomes they cannot control*

Submission strengthens leadership because it keeps leaders aligned with reality rather than ego, especially in fast-changing, uncertain environments.

Holding Plans Firmly - But Not Tightly

Healthy leaders distinguish between direction and attachment.
They hold direction firmly:

- *Purpose*
- *Values*
- *Desired outcomes*

They hold tactics loosely:

- *Methods*
- *Timelines*
- *Approaches*

This balance allows leaders to remain steady without becoming stubborn. A strategic plan may begin the year clearly defined, yet require adjustment mid-year as people, conditions, or information change. Wisdom is not found in rigid adherence, but in faithful responsiveness.

When leaders confuse firmness with inflexibility, they lose effectiveness. When they confuse submission with hesitation, they lose momentum. Wisdom holds both.

Planning as a Spiritual and Practical Discipline

Planning with submission shapes leadership character.
It cultivates:
Thoughtfulness over impulse
Dependence over self-reliance
Clarity without arrogance
Confidence without presumption

Leaders who submit their plans invite wisdom beyond their own perspective. They plan diligently, then remain attentive to what unfolds.

A Leadership Practice

Practice: Plan and Release

Reflect honestly:

- *What plans am I currently holding too tightly?*
- *Where might flexibility improve outcomes?*
- *Have I invited counsel into my planning process?*
- What would it look like to commit this plan and release control of the outcome?

Write one plan you are working on.
Identify what must remain firm and what must remain flexible.

Closing Reflection

Planning is responsible.
Submission is wise.

Leaders who plan with submission avoid the twin dangers of drift and domination. They move forward with clarity, humility, and adaptability.
In leadership, the goal is not to control outcomes but to steward direction faithfully.

Commit to the LORD whatever you do, and he will establish your plans.

Proverbs 16:3

Planning shapes direction. ***Justice determines whether that direction is trusted.***

In the final chapter, we turn to justice, fairness, and trust - the visible outcome of leadership that has been carried with care from the inside out.

Chapter Ten

Justice, Fairness, and Trust

Trust is the quiet currency of leadership.

It is built slowly, spent quickly, and replenished only through consistent fairness over time. Leaders may have authority by position, but trust is granted by people and justice is one of the primary ways it is earned.

Fair leadership is not accidental.
It is intentional, disciplined, and visible.

Why Fairness Matters More Than Leaders Realize

Leaders make decisions daily that affect people differently:

- Assignments
- Opportunities
- Feedback
- Consequences
- Recognition

When fairness is absent or even perceived to be absent - trust erodes.
People may comply, but they stop committing.

Scripture speaks directly to this leadership responsibility:

"Honest scales delight the LORD,
but dishonest weights are detestable to him."
- Proverbs 11:1

Justice is not an abstract virtue.
It is expressed through systems, decisions, and consistency.

Fairness Is Consistency Applied with Wisdom

Fairness does not mean treating everyone identically.
It means applying standards consistently and impartially, while exercising discernment where circumstances differ.
Unfair leadership often shows up as:

- *Favoritism*
- *Inconsistent enforcement of rules*
- *Special exceptions for those in proximity to power*
- *Silence when correction is uncomfortable*

Over time, these behaviors communicate something leaders may never say out loud:
"Rules are flexible depending on who you are."
That message destroys trust.

The Cost of Favoritism

Favoritism is one of the fastest ways to fracture leadership credibility.
When leaders show preference intentionally or not,they:

- *Undermine morale*
- *Create suspicion*
- *Discourage excellence*
- *Invite quiet disengagement*

People may stop raising concerns, offering ideas, or investing fully-not because they don't care, but because they no longer trust the system to be fair.

Justice restores confidence.

In my experience, leaders often underestimate how quickly perceived favoritism - not just actual bias can unravel years of goodwill.

Transparent Standards Build Confidence

Trust grows when people understand:

- *What is expected*
- *How decisions are made*
- *What standards apply*
- *What consequences follow*

Transparency does not require explaining every decision. It requires leaders to be clear, consistent, and principled.

When leaders lead this way:

- *Accountability feels fair, not personal*
- *Correction feels constructive, not punitive*
- *Authority feels protective, not threatening*

Justice humanizes leadership.

Fair Leaders Create Safe Environments

Fairness creates psychological safety.
When people trust leadership to act justly, they are more willing to:

- *Speak honestly*
- *Take responsibility*
- *Admit mistakes*
- *Grow through feedback*

Justice does not eliminate conflict.
It ensures conflict is handled with dignity.
Fair systems applied consistently, protect both people and the structure that supports them.

A Leadership Practice

Practice: Fairness Check

Ask yourself:

- Are standards applied consistently across people and situations?
- Where might familiarity or proximity be influencing my judgment?
- Do people understand how decisions are made?
- How would those affected describe the fairness of my leadership?

Invite honest feedback where possible.
Fair leadership is strengthened through accountability.

Closing Reflection

Justice is not optional for leadership credibility.
Fair leaders do not eliminate disappointment - but they prevent distrust.
Over time, justice builds confidence in leadership systems and stability in culture.

Leadership that is fair earns loyalty not through favoritism, but through integrity

*The LORD detests dishonest scales,
but accurate weights find favor
with him.*

Proverbs 11:1

Leadership Self-Assessment

Leading with Care

This assessment is designed to help you pause, reflect, and realign. Answer honestly. There are no scores to impress-only clarity to gain.

Instructions

Read each statement carefully. Rate yourself based on current behavior, not intention.

Scale:
1 = Rarely true
2 = Sometimes true
3 = Often true
4 = Consistently true

Section 1: Care & Responsibility

Statement	1	2	3	4
I consider how my decisions affect people before acting	☐	☐	☐	☐
I feel responsible for the impact of my leadership	☐	☐	☐	☐
I prioritize long-term outcomes over short-term convenience	☐	☐	☐	☐

Reflection:
Where might I need to lead more thoughtfully or responsibly?

Section 2: Character & Integrity

Statement	1	2	3	4
My actions align with my stated values	☐	☐	☐	☐
I hold myself to the same standards I expect of others	☐	☐	☐	☐
I act with integrity even when no one is watching	☐	☐	☐	☐

Reflection:
Where might small compromises be forming?

Section 3: Humility & Self-Leadership

Statement	1	2	3	4
I invite counsel before major decisions	☐	☐	☐	☐
I respond thoughtfully under pressure	☐	☐	☐	☐
I govern my emotions rather than react impulsively	☐	☐	☐	☐

Reflection:
What situations most test my humility or emotional discipline?

Section 4: Discipline & Consistency

Statement	1	2	3	4
I prepare consistently for my leadership responsibilities	☐	☐	☐	☐
I follow through on commitments	☐	☐	☐	☐
I model the discipline I expect from others	☐	☐	☐	☐

Reflection:
What one habit would most strengthen my leadership?

Section 5: Communication & Fairness

Statement	1	2	3	4
My words generally bring clarity and stability	☐	☐	☐	☐
I apply standards consistently and fairly	☐	☐	☐	☐
People trust my decisions even when they disagree	☐	☐	☐	☐

Reflection:
How might others experience my leadership differently than I intend?

Closing Reflection

Answer in one or two sentences:

What is one area where I need to lead with greater care in this season?

____

____

Commitment (Optional but Recommended)

One leadership adjustment I will make this month:

Date: _______________
Signature (optional): __________________________________

How to Use This Assessment

Complete it monthly or quarterly

Discuss it with a mentor or trusted peer

Use it alongside this playbook for reflection and growth

Leadership strengthens when reflection becomes routine.

Epilogue

Choosing to Lead with Care

If you have made it this far, you are already doing something many leaders never do. You are pausing to think about how you lead, not just what you achieve.

That pause matters.

Leadership is not sustained by intention alone. It is sustained by the choices leaders make when no one is applauding, when pressure is present, and when outcomes are uncertain. This playbook was not written to create perfect leaders, but responsible ones.

Care is not an accessory to leadership.

It is the condition that keeps leadership from becoming reckless.

Throughout these pages, one idea has remained consistent. Leadership carries weight. Influence affects people. Decisions leave marks. Words linger. Habits compound. Fairness builds, or erodes, trust. None of this is theoretical. It is lived daily.

To lead with care is to accept that responsibility fully.

It means:

- Choosing character over convenience
- Stewarding authority rather than owning it
- Exercising power with restraint

- Governing your inner life before shaping others
- Speaking with intention
- Practicing discipline consistently
- Planning wisely without clinging to control
- Leading fairly, even when it costs you

This kind of leadership will not always be celebrated. It will not always be fast. It will not always be easy. But it will be stable, trustworthy, and enduring.

Care-centered leadership does not demand perfection. It demands honesty. It asks leaders to remain teachable, accountable, and willing to reflect, especially when leadership becomes complex.

You will make mistakes. All leaders do. The difference will not be whether you err, but how you respond. Whether you correct course, tell the truth, and recommit to leading responsibly.

If there is one question worth carrying forward, let it be this:
Who has been entrusted to my leadership, and how well am I caring for that responsibility?
Return to that question often.

Leadership is not measured only by results achieved, but by people strengthened, trust preserved, and influence exercised with wisdom.

Choose to lead with care.
Not occasionally, but consistently.
That choice will shape more than outcomes.
It will shape lives.

Bibliography

Scripture

The Holy Bible, English Standard Version. Wheaton, IL: Crossway.

The Holy Bible, New International Version. Grand Rapids, MI: Zondervan. (All Scripture references in this book are drawn from these translations unless otherwise noted.)

Biblical Wisdom and Formation

Keller, Timothy. Every Good Endeavor: Connecting Your Work to God's Work. New York: Penguin Books, 2014.

Peterson, Eugene H. A Long Obedience in the Same Direction: Discipleship in an Instant Society. Downers Grove, IL: InterVarsity Press, 2000.

Wright, N. T. After You Believe: Why Christian Character Matters. New York: HarperOne, 2010.

Willard, Dallas. The Spirit of the Disciplines: Understanding How God Changes Lives. New York: HarperOne, 1999.

Leadership, Stewardship, and Responsibility

Drucker, Peter F. The Effective Executive. New York: HarperBusiness, 2006.

Heifetz, Ronald A., and Marty Linsky. Leadership on the Line: Staying Alive through the Dangers of Leading. Boston: Harvard Business School Press, 2002.

Greenleaf, Robert K. Servant Leadership: A Journey into the Nature of Legitimate Power and Greatness. New York: Paulist Press, 1977.

Maxwell, John C. The 21 Irrefutable Laws of Leadership. Nashville, TN: Thomas Nelson, 2007.

Character, Discipline, and Self-Leadership

Covey, Stephen R. The 7 Habits of Highly Effective People. New York: Free Press, 2004.

Goleman, Daniel. Emotional Intelligence: Why It Can Matter More Than IQ. New York: Bantam Books, 1995.

Brown, Brené. Dare to Lead. New York: Random House, 2018.

Sinek, Simon. Leaders Eat Last: Why Some Teams Pull Together and Others Don't. New York: Portfolio, 2014.

Workplace Culture and Communication

Gallup. State of the Global Workplace: 2023 Report. Washington, DC: Gallup Press, 2023.

Author's Related Work

Olaleye, Lanre B. The Five Factor Formula. Tampa, FL: Gatekeeper Press, 2025.

Olaleye, Lanre B. Insight at Work. McKinney, TX: LBO Publishing, 2026

Note on Sources
This bibliography reflects sources that inform the philosophy, formation, and leadership posture presented in this book. The work itself prioritizes Scripture-anchored wisdom, lived leadership experience, and practical application over extensive citation.

www.ingramcontent.com/pod-product-compliance
Lightning Source LLC
LaVergne TN
LVHW010951110826
845149LV00015B/3294

9798995815044